Contents

Sitting Bull

Sandra Woodcock

Published in association with The Basic Skills Agency

Hodder & Stoughton

A MEMBER OF THE HODDER HEADLINE GROUP

Acknowledgements

Cover photo: AKG.

Photos: pp. 5, 7, 11, 14, 16, 18 Corbis-Bettmann; p. 20 Library of Congress/Corbis; p. 24 UPI/Corbis.

Orders: please contact Bookpoint Ltd, 39 Milton Park, Abingdon, Oxon OX14 4TD. Telephone: (44) 01235 400414, Fax: (44) 01235 400454. Lines are open from 9.00–6.00, Monday to Saturday, with a 24 hour message answering service. Email address: orders@bookpoint.co.uk

British Library Cataloguing in Publication Data
A catalogue record for this title is available from The British Library

ISBN 0 340 74725 0

First published 1999
Impression number   10 9 8 7 6 5 4 3 2 1
Year   2004 2003 2002 2001 2000 1999

Typeset by Fakenham Photosetting Ltd, Fakenham, Norfolk.
Printed in Great Britain for Hodder & Stoughton Educational, a division of Hodder Headline Plc, 338 Euston Road, London NW1 3BH by Redwood Books, Trowbridge, Wiltshire.

Sitting Bull was an American Indian chief.
He was a leader of an Indian tribe
called the Sioux.

The Sioux lived on the Great Plains
of North America.
The Great Plains were grasslands.
They were home to herds of buffalo.
The Sioux lived by hunting the buffalo.

In Sitting Bull's lifetime,
white Americans came
to the lands of the Sioux.
They came looking for gold.
They made roads and railways.
They built army bases, called forts.
And they upset the Indian way of life.

The Indians attacked the white settlers.
The settlers attacked the Indians.
It was a war between two ways of life.

1 The Life of a Sioux Indian

The Sioux did not live in one place
but moved around.
They were nomads.
They followed the buffalo.
They lived in tents made from cloth
or buffalo skins, called tepees.

The Sioux lived by hunting and fighting.
When Sitting Bull was a boy,
he went hunting with the men of the tribe.
He had to learn to ride a horse
and later, to use a gun.
He had to prove his manhood.
He had to fight in wars with other tribes.
He had to kill.
Young men of the Sioux tribe
had to prove that they were brave.
They had to show that they could stand pain.
They had to do the Sun Dance.

In the Sun Dance,
the men would cut themselves with knives.
They wanted to show how brave they were.

The Sioux men were brought up to fight.
They would fight for their lands and their people.
They would fight other Indian tribes.
The Sioux were strong and fierce,
but they also loved family life.
They never hit their children.
They cared for their women.
The family was important to the Sioux.

Like all Sioux, Sitting Bull loved freedom.
He loved the wide open space of the Great Plains.
The Sioux hunted and killed animals to live,
but they had a great love for nature.
The Sioux way of life
was different from that of the settlers.

The Indian way of life.

2 Gold

In the 1850s, settlers found gold in Montana.
To get to the gold they had to make a trail.
It crossed Indian lands.
As the settlers used the trail,
the Indians attacked them.
So the US army built forts along the trail.
A Sioux chief, called Red Cloud,
attacked the forts.
He led the Indians in a war for two years
to try and stop the settlers.

In 1869, Red Cloud signed a treaty
– a special agreement –
with the US government.
The Sioux lands would be left alone,
but at a price.
The Sioux had to move to South Dakota.
They had to live on certain land,
called a reservation.

Settlers crossing Indian land.

Many Indians did not want to.
It would mean losing their freedom.

Red Cloud moved to the reservation.
He was now a peace chief
and worked with the US government.

Two other Sioux chiefs
did not want to take their people to reservations.
They were Crazy Horse and Sitting Bull.
They wanted to fight for their freedom.

3 The War for the Black Hills

In 1874, settlers found gold in the Black Hills.
The Black Hills belonged to the Indians.
But now there was a rush to get the gold.
The Indians would be in the way.
The US government wanted the Indians to move.
They wanted them to live on reservations.
They wanted them to become farmers.

The Indians now looked to Sitting Bull
and Crazy Horse to help them.

The Black Hills were important to the Indians.
They were a place to go and pray.
The Indians could not understand
why the white men wanted gold.
They called it 'the yellow metal
that makes the whites go crazy'.

The Indians believed Sitting Bull
could see into the future.

As the war for the Black Hills was about to start,
Sitting Bull did the Sun Dance for 24 hours.
He made a hundred cuts into his arms.
He had a dream.
He saw white soldiers,
falling upside down from the sky.
The Indians believed
they would win a great battle.

General George Custer was a US army leader.
He was sent to track down Indians.
He found a camp
near the Little Bighorn River.

General George Custer with his scouts.

Custer thought he could deal with these Indians.
He had 655 men with him.
But the Indians (Sioux and Cheyenne tribes)
had at least 2,500.
They were led by Sitting Bull and Crazy Horse.

In the Battle of the Little Bighorn, 25 June 1876,
Custer was killed.
The Indians killed 300 US soldiers.
This was the Indians' great battle.

But in the end
the whites were bound to win the war.
They had more men and more guns.

4 Canada

After the Battle of the Little Bighorn,
the settlers wanted revenge.
They made the Indians suffer.
They killed men, women and children.
Many others died of cold and hunger.
Sitting Bull and Crazy Horse
went away to the north.

The US government
made the Reservation Indians sign a treaty.
The treaty gave The Black Hills to the settlers.
The herds of buffalo had gone.
The Indians had no food.
They needed money from the government.
If they did not go into reservations,
they would starve.

The soldiers of the US army chased the Indians
everywhere they went.
They wanted them all on reservations.
Crazy Horse gave in to the soldiers.
He was killed by a soldier's bayonet.

The US government and the Indians.

But still, Sitting Bull
would not give up his freedom.
He and his people went to Canada.
He was now the only Indian leader
who had not given up.

The US government did not like it.
Sitting Bull was now on British land.
They could not force him to leave Canada.
They tried to talk him round.
But Sitting Bull stayed in Canada for four years.
The government of Canada
would not give the Indians land.

Life was hard.

In the bad winter of 1880,
many Sioux horses froze to death.
Now they had no chance.
They were poor and hungry.
Sitting Bull had to leave Canada
and give himself up to the US government.
He went to Standing Rock Reservation.

Sitting Bull in 1881.

5 On Tour

Sitting Bull was still a problem.
Many Indians looked to him as a leader.
He told them not to sell land
from their reservations.
He warned them not to trust the settlers.

The government wanted him out of the way.

They fixed a tour for him.
In 1884 he went to 15 cities.
The next year he went on tour
with Buffalo Bill's Wild West Show.
Crowds came to see him.
He signed photos for them.
When they gave him money,
he gave it away to the poor children he saw.

Sitting Bull with Buffalo Bill.

Buffalo Bill wanted him to tour Europe.
But Sitting Bull said no.
He went back to Standing Rock.

The government was still trying
to make the Indians sell their land.
The whites wanted
to make the reservation smaller.
Sitting Bull did his best to stop this.
But in the end the government had its way.
The Sioux lands were now smaller than ever.

Sitting Bull was angry.

He had another vision.
It was about his own death.
He said the Sioux would kill him.

The Ghost Dance.

6 The Ghost Dance

Sitting Bull felt the Indians had lost everything.
Their way of life was ending.
They did not even have their pride.

In 1890, an Indian called Kicking Bear
came to see Sitting Bull.
He told him there was a new religion for Indians.
He said the Indians must do a new dance.
It was called the Ghost Dance.
If the Indians did this dance,
then they would be saved.
The white men would die.
All the Indians from the past
would come back to earth.
Herds of buffalo would come back.
Wild horses would come back.
The Indians would live free,
as they had done before.

On some reservations
they were dancing the Ghost Dance.

Sitting Bull said
that white men did not like the Ghost Dance.
Soldiers were shooting Indians because of it.

Then Kicking Bear said
the Indians must wear Ghost shirts.
They had magic signs on them.
The Ghost Shirts would stop
the white men's bullets.
Sitting Bull did not believe all of this.
But he let Kicking Bear stay.
He let him show the people the new dance.

The government was afraid of the Ghost Dance.
They wanted to end the old Indian way of life.
The Ghost Dance was in all the reservations.
The settlers thought it would make trouble.
If there was trouble,
Sitting Bull would be a leader.
Soldiers were sent to get Sitting Bull.
He could help the government
to stop the Ghost Dance.

On 15 December 1890,
some Indians
who worked as policemen for the settlers
came to Sitting Bull's cabin.
Sitting Bull was ready to go with them
but someone tried to stop them taking him.

A gun went off.
Then there was another shot.
Sitting Bull was shot in the head.
His dream had come true:
he had been killed by a Sioux Indian.

The death of Sitting Bull.

7 The End Of A Dream

After Sitting Bull died, his people were afraid.
They ran away to the camp of Big Foot,
who was another Sioux chief.
But US soldiers chased them.

They found the Indians
at a place called 'Wounded Knee'.
There were 120 men
and 230 women and children.
The chief, Big Foot, was very ill.
He put up a white flag.

The soldiers told the Indians to give up their guns.
One Indian fired his gun.
Then the soldiers began firing.

Their big guns tore the tents to pieces.
Women and children were shot
as well as the men.
Many were shot as they tried to run away.
Few had weapons.

It is not clear how many died
but it may have been 300.

After the shooting, a snowstorm began.
Many of the dead were left
lying on the ground.
'Wounded Knee' was the end
of the Indian fight for freedom.
After this, many more gave up hope.

Sitting Bull had not lived to see
the killings at 'Wounded Knee'.
All his life, he had tried
to save the Indian way of life.
He had tried to save the Indian lands.
He was one of the last Indians
to make a stand for freedom.

After 'Wounded Knee',
the last Indians went into the reservations.
A dream had died.